# IMAGES OF
# MADISON COUNTY

#### PHOTOGRAPHY BY
#### STEPHEN KIRKPATRICK

WRITTEN BY MARLO CARTER KIRKPATRICK

*[signature]*

FOREWORD BY CONGRESSMAN CHIP PICKERING

# Thy Marvelous Works

102 PROPRIETOR'S POINT, MADISON, MS 39110, 1-888-471-4040, WWW.KIRKPATRICKWILDLIFE.COM

*WRITTEN BY:* MARLO CARTER KIRKPATRICK    *DESIGNER:* HEIDI FLYNN ALLEN    *PROOFREADER:* SISSY YERGER    *PRINTER:* EVERBEST, CHINA

    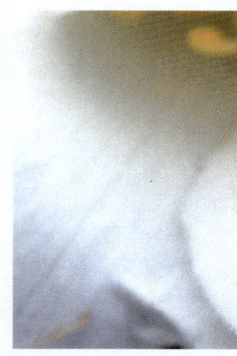

*(previous page)*

**INTO THE LIGHT**
December 2003
*17-35mm, f8@1/250*

*The rising sun burns life into a cold, foggy morning.*

IMAGE SCANNING: DIGITAL IMAGING GROUP    SPECIAL THANKS TO: BILL RAY, BANKPLUS    ISBN # 0-9619353-0-8    © 2006 STEPHEN KIRKPATRICK

 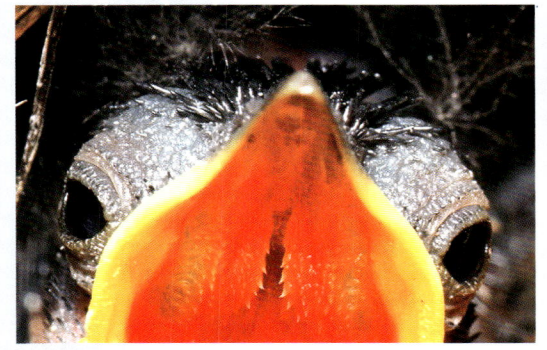  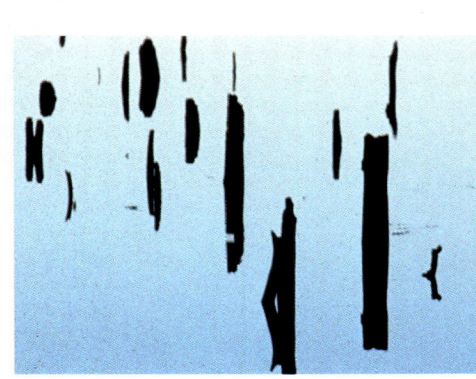

### RESERVOIR DAWN
April 1988
*24mm, f8@1/60*

*The yet-to-appear sun paints the skies over the Ross Barnett Reservoir.*

**MANNSDALE VIEW**
November 2005
*17–35mm, w/polarizer f11@1/30*

*Despite its rapid growth, Madison County is still marked by tall trees and wide open spaces.*

**PINING AWAY**
January 2006
*17–35mm, f11@1/15*
*Pine trees stand watch in the fog.*

**MORNING COMMUTE**
September 2002
*500mm, f4@1/1000*

*Canada geese leave their resting place and head out for the day.*

**CARDINAL CLASSIC**
March 2006
*500mm w/2x TC, f4@1/60*

*A male cardinal in a blooming crabapple makes for a vivid portrait.*

# FOREWORD

In 2003, my wife, Leisha, and I moved from Virginia back to Mississippi, settling our family in rural Madison County. We wanted to raise our children in Mississippi and Madison County offered a rare combination of city conveniences and nature's tranquilities, literally in our own backyard.

Here, my family and I explore the unspoiled fields and forests that surround our farm, sharing wilderness adventures that make us appreciate the expansive natural world surrounding us while bringing us closer personally to one another.

I grew up hunting and fishing in Mississippi's woodlands and wetlands, and those pursuits remain a passion today. My wife often jokes that were I not a congressman, I would probably be a hunting guide. I've passed that same love of the outdoors on to my five sons. Will, Ross, Jack, Asher, and Harper are avid hunters, joining me in search of deer, turkey, and ducks. My boys have also discovered that Mississippi's natural beauty is always in season. There's not a day on the calendar that can't be made more special by a simple walk in the woods.

Most importantly, our time together in Madison County has instilled in each of my sons a deeper love not only for nature, but for its Creator. In those quiet moments outdoors, surrounded by the trees, the wind, the waters, and the wildlife that He formed, we can truly feel the presence of God.

In these pages, Stephen Kirkpatrick has captured the beauty of nature and the awesome power of nature's Creator. When I'm immersed in the hustle and bustle of Washington, I have only to peruse the pages of *Images of Madison County* to find myself once again lost in those tranquil fields and forests.

*Images of Madison County* captures the beauty, the wonder, and the sheer joy that make me feel blessed to call Madison County, Mississippi, home.

*Chip Pickering*

CONGRESSMAN CHIP PICKERING

**MOONSHINE**
June 2004
*60mm, f2.8@1/60*

*A cypress tree in the moonrise creates an intoxicating atmosphere.*

**WALNUT REFLECTIONS**
March 1998
*24mm, f22@1/8*

*Treetops reflected in quiet Walnut Creek.*

**IN THE SHALLOWS**
November 1984
*300mm, f4.5@1/250*

*A great egret searches for fish along the shallow reservoir shore.*

**COLORFUL GATHERING**
August 2005
*180mm, f8@1/125*

*A tiger swallowtail gathers nectar among blazing star.*

**BIG BLACK GLOW**
November 2005
*17-35mm w/split ND, f2.8@4 sec.*

*The Big Black River glows at dusk.*

**OAK AT DAWN**
October 2005
*17-35mm, f8@1/30*

*Morning's first rays shine through
the branches of a lone oak.*

**BLUE FLAG BOUNTY**
June 1999
*24mm, f16@1/30*

*Blue flag irises wave against a backdrop of blooming willow.*

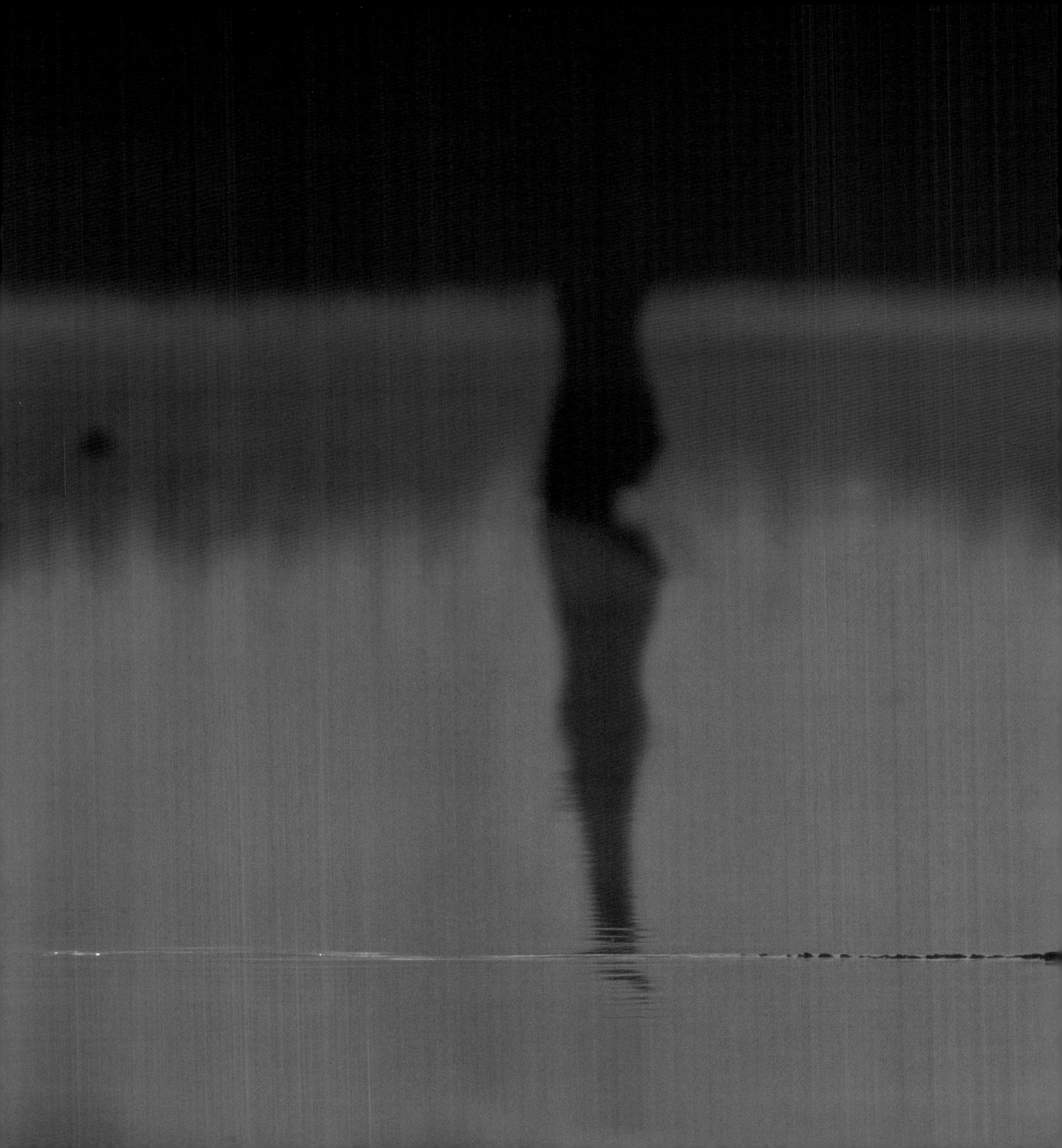

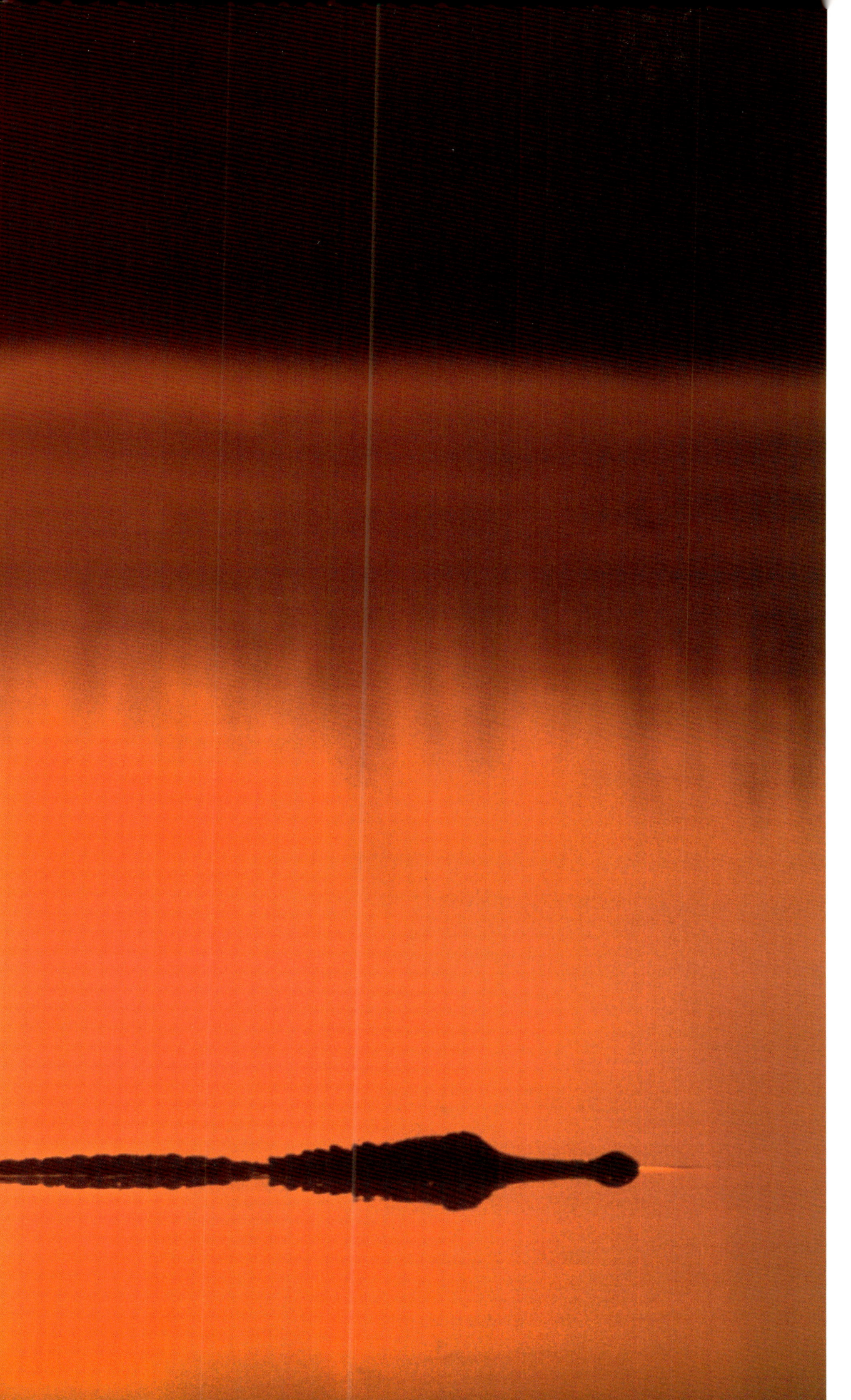

### SUNRISE CRUISE
May 2005
*500mm, f4@1/125*

*An alligator cruises the Pearl River swamp at sunrise.*

### STRUTTER
April 1982
*300mm, f4.5@1/250*

*A double-bearded eastern wild turkey struts for attention.*

# THERE'S NO PLACE LIKE HOME

Madison County, Mississippi, is close to my heart. It's not only the place I call home, but also the place where I launched my career as a wildlife and nature photographer. I picked up my first camera in 1981 and the natural beauty of Madison County was the first thing I saw through its lens.

For the next several years, I taught myself the art and craft of photography in Madison County's forests, lakes, and fields. As a budding wildlife photographer, I dreamed of working in exotic locales, of photographing lions on the Serengeti or anacondas in the Amazon, but I was too broke to go any farther than the pastures of Flora or the waters of the Ross Barnett Reservoir.

But as I soon discovered, everything I needed to capture a moving photograph—light, scenery, subjects ranging from majestic bucks to dew-covered butterflies—was right there, in my own backyard. I stopped longing to take an ordinary photograph of an extraordinary subject, and focused instead on capturing extraordinary photographs of the familiar.

Since those early years, my photography career has at times taken me far from the familiar southern swamps and well-known woodlands where I first honed my craft. But no matter what I see of the rest of the world, I never tire of working in my own little corner of it, and I've never been disappointed by what Madison County has to offer.

The images on these pages were all shot within the 720 square miles of the county I call home. The earliest photo is of an eastern wild turkey taken in 1982, less than one year after I first picked up a camera. Every year since is represented by at least one photo in this book.

No matter how long ago they were taken or where I was standing (or hanging, hiding, wading, crawling, or crouching) when I pressed the shutter release, every image stirs a vivid memory of a special moment in Madison County. And every shot makes me realize the truth in the old cliché—there really is no place like home.

STEPHEN KIRKPATRICK

*September 2006*

**DEW DROP IN**
September 2003
*60mm, f11@1/30*

*A moth clings to the dew-covered hairs of a foxtail in the early morning light.*

**FALL GOLD**
November 2000
*180mm, f8@1/125*

*Fall leaves glow in the late evening sun.*

**WEB OF PEARLS**
October 2004
*60mm, f8@1/4*

*A dew-covered spider web offers a veiled view of the Pearl River on a foggy morning.*

**MISTY MOONSET**
October 2004
*180mm, f4@1/60*
*The full moon sets over a quiet field.*

**GLORIOUS PERCH**
December 2004
*500mm, f4@1/250*

*A red-tailed hawk crowned with a glorious glow.*

**WINGING IT**
February 2003
*500mm, f4@1/1000*

*White pelicans depart their resting place.*

**SUMAC SYMPHONY**
October 1991
*105mm, f8@1/60*

*The changing colors of sumac form
a harmonious composition.*

**LUNCH BREAK**
June 2004
*500mm, f4@1/30*

*A female indigo bunting feeds a katydid to her young.*

**SPRING GREENING**
April 2006
*17–35mm w/polarizer, f8@1/30*

*Spring leaves are the purest green of the year.*

# MADISON COUNTY
*Portrait of a Place*

When it was established in 1828, Madison County originally covered more than 4,000 square miles. Over the next three decades portions of that land were allocated to other counties. Its present-day boundaries were established in 1859, with 720 scenic square miles permanently designated as Madison County.

Bordered by the Pearl River to the east and the Big Black River to the west, Madison County is sometimes referred to as "the land between two rivers." The county's interior is a mix of fields, forests, lakes, and creeks. Add the 33,000-acre Ross Barnett Reservoir and the protected wilderness that surrounds the Natchez Trace Parkway, and the opportunity for outdoor adventures in Madison County is endless.

Madison County is one of the fastest growing counties in Mississippi, and yet the area retains its natural beauty. Whether they live in a new subdivision, a quiet country cabin, or on a generations-old family farm, residents here seem to appreciate that one of the things that makes Madison County so desirable is its flora and fauna. In Madison County, there is still the opportunity to hear a bird sing, to stumble upon a brilliant bouquet of wildflowers, to catch a fleeting glimpse of a whitetail, all in one's own backyard.

To some, Madison County is just another of the 82 counties that make up the state of Mississippi. But for those who look closer, Madison County is a rare blend of modern growth and timeless natural beauty.

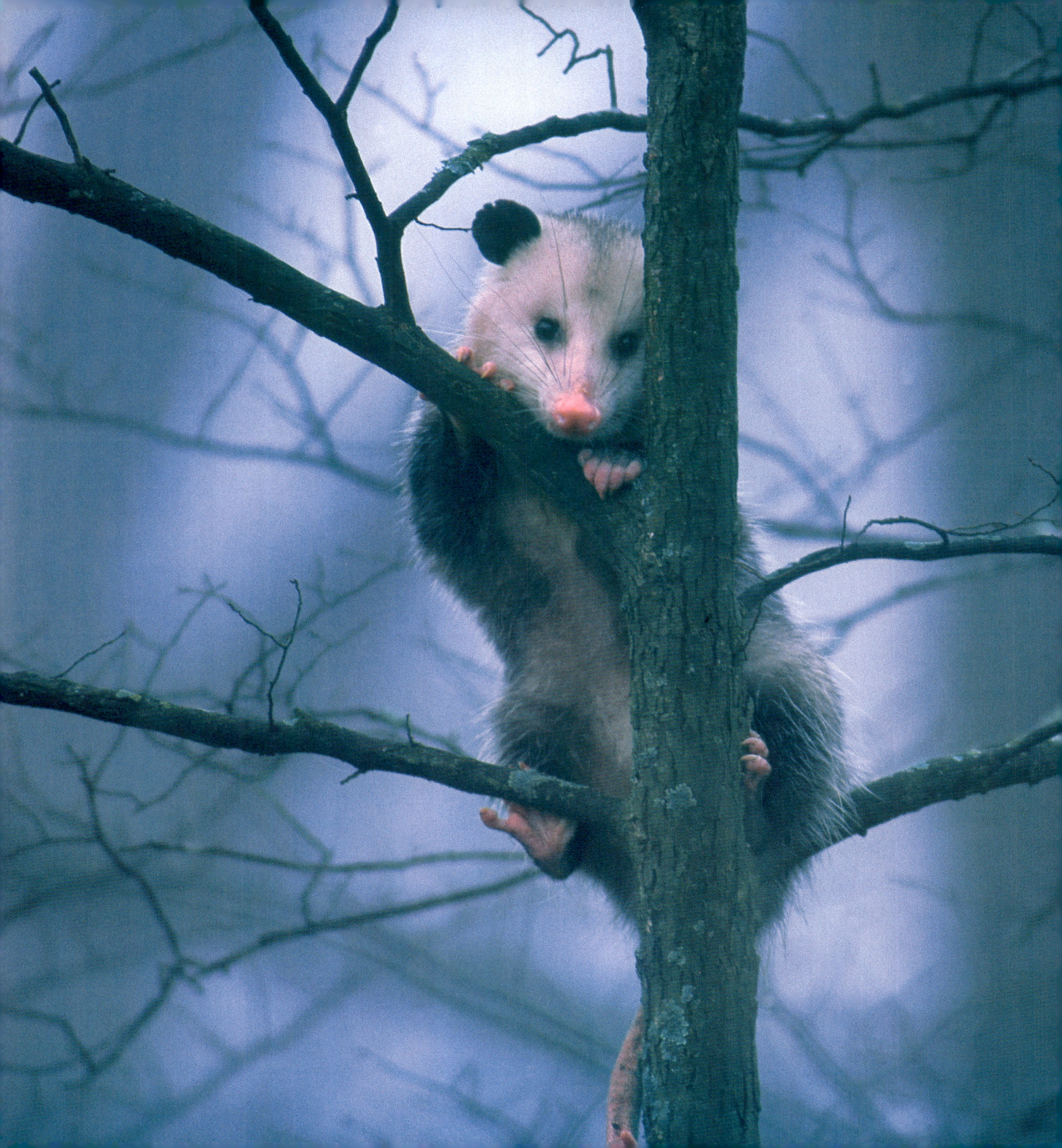

**BRANCHING OUT**
February 2005
*500mm, f4@1/60*

*A foggy morning finds a young opossum caught in an awkward position.*

**GREYSTONE PATRIARCH**
November 1987
*400mm, f3.5@1/500*

*A golden sunset burns bright behind the lone tree on a hill.*

**BLACK-EYED BUNCH**
June 2004
*17-35mm, f22@1/2*

*Black-eyed Susans bloom near the wood's edge.*

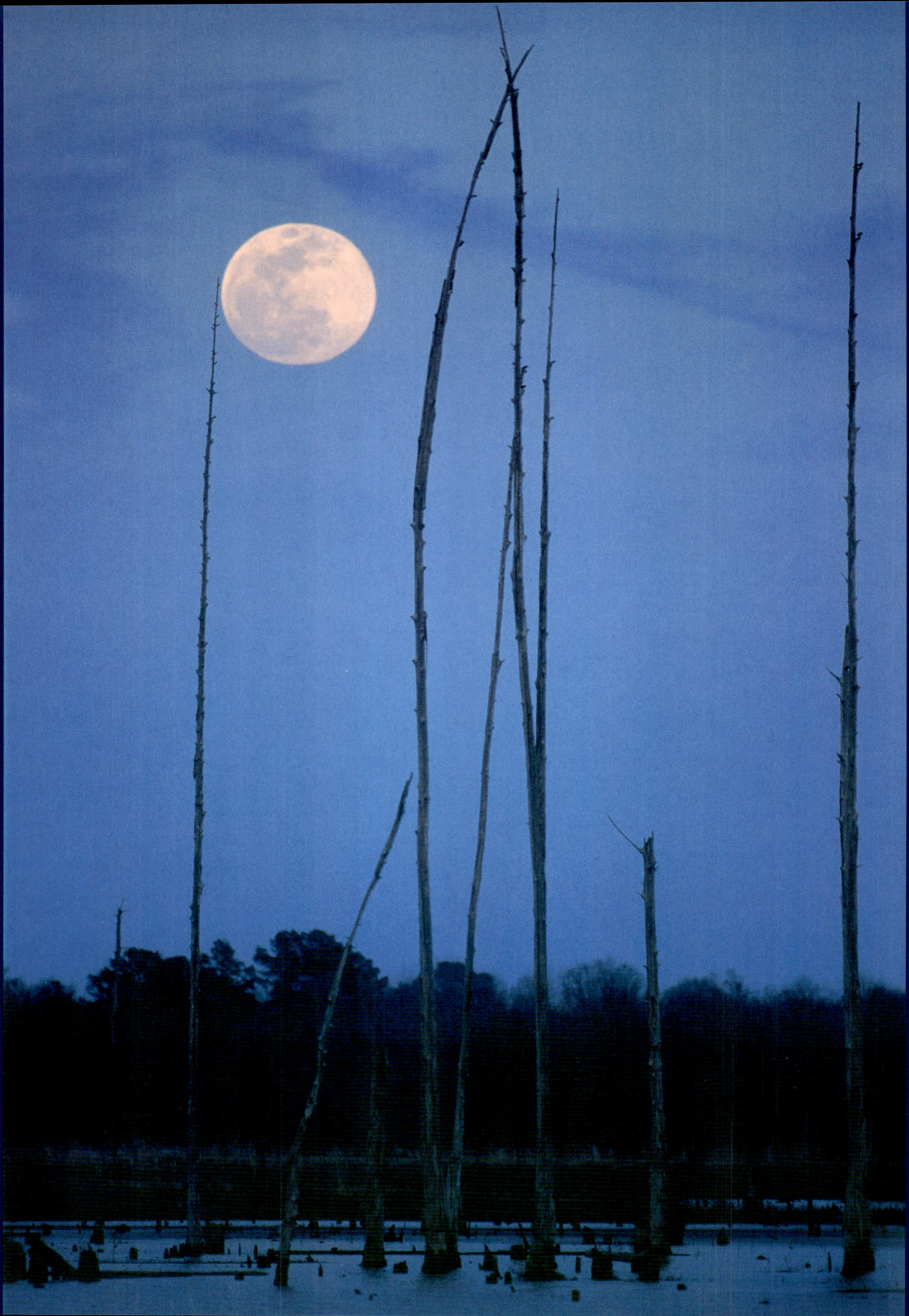

**PEARL MOON**
February 2001
*180mm, f2.8@1/4*

*A full moon rises over the Pearl River swamp.*

**CELESTIAL GLOW**
November 2004
*180mm, f4@1/125*

*Sunset colors the clouds.*

43

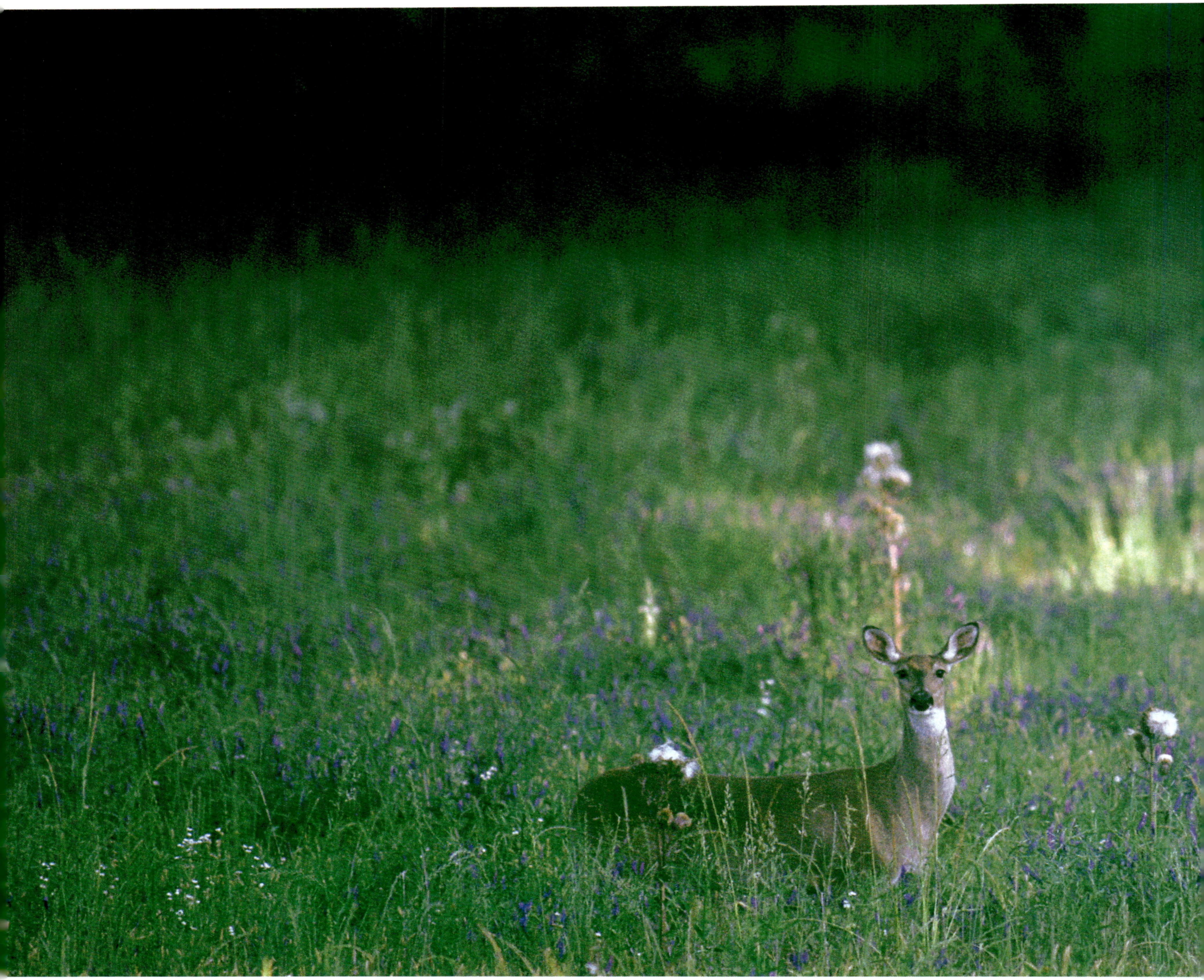

**MAY FREEZE**
May 1990
*400mm, f3.5@1/125*
*White-tailed does stand motionless in a field of vetch.*

'PILLAR PATTERN
July 1995
*105mm, f16@1/8*

*Patterns on a hornworm's back blend into the leaves.*

MORNING PRAYERS
August 2003
*60mm, f11@1/15*

*A praying mantis awaits its prey against a backdrop of vivid ironweed.*

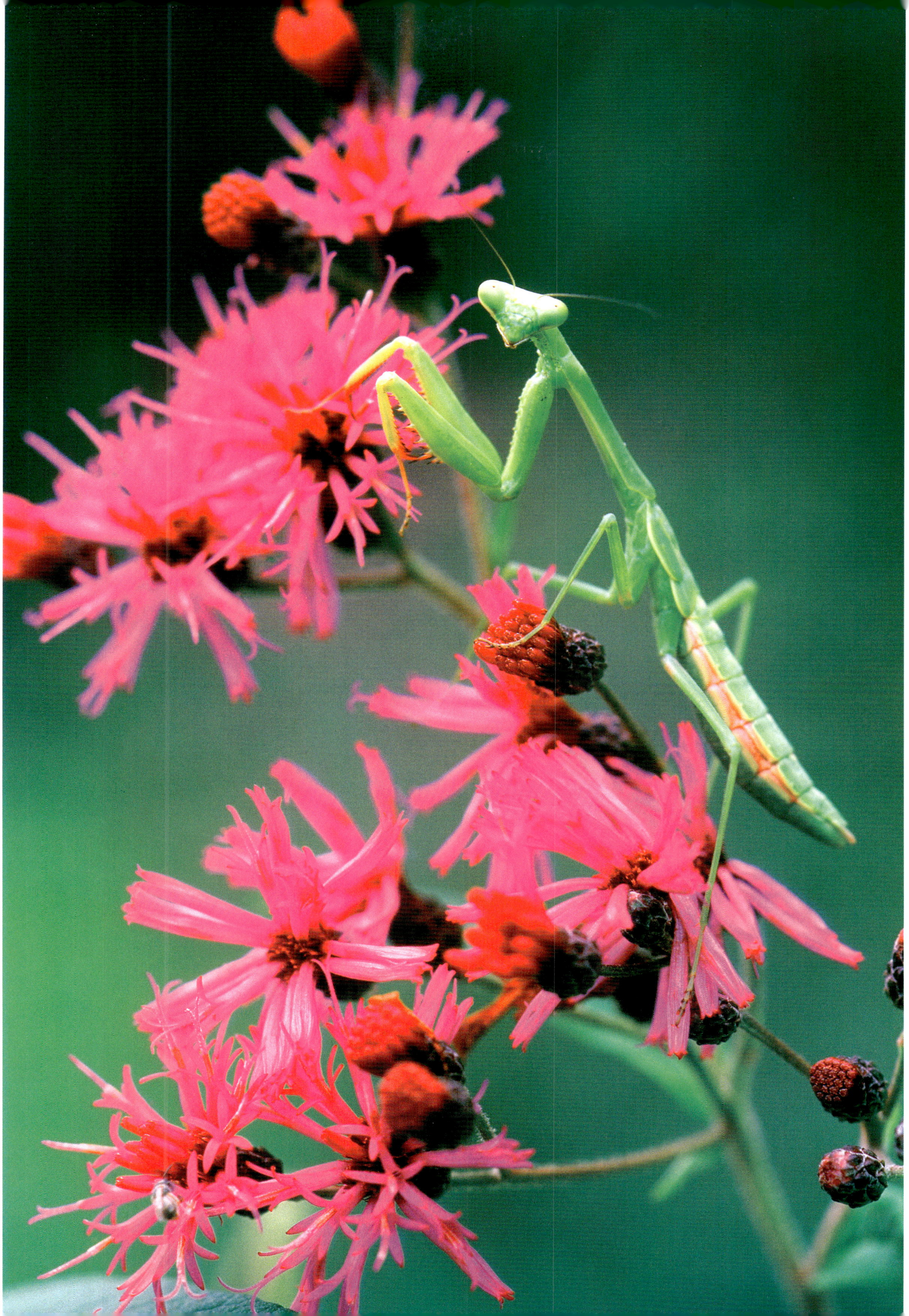

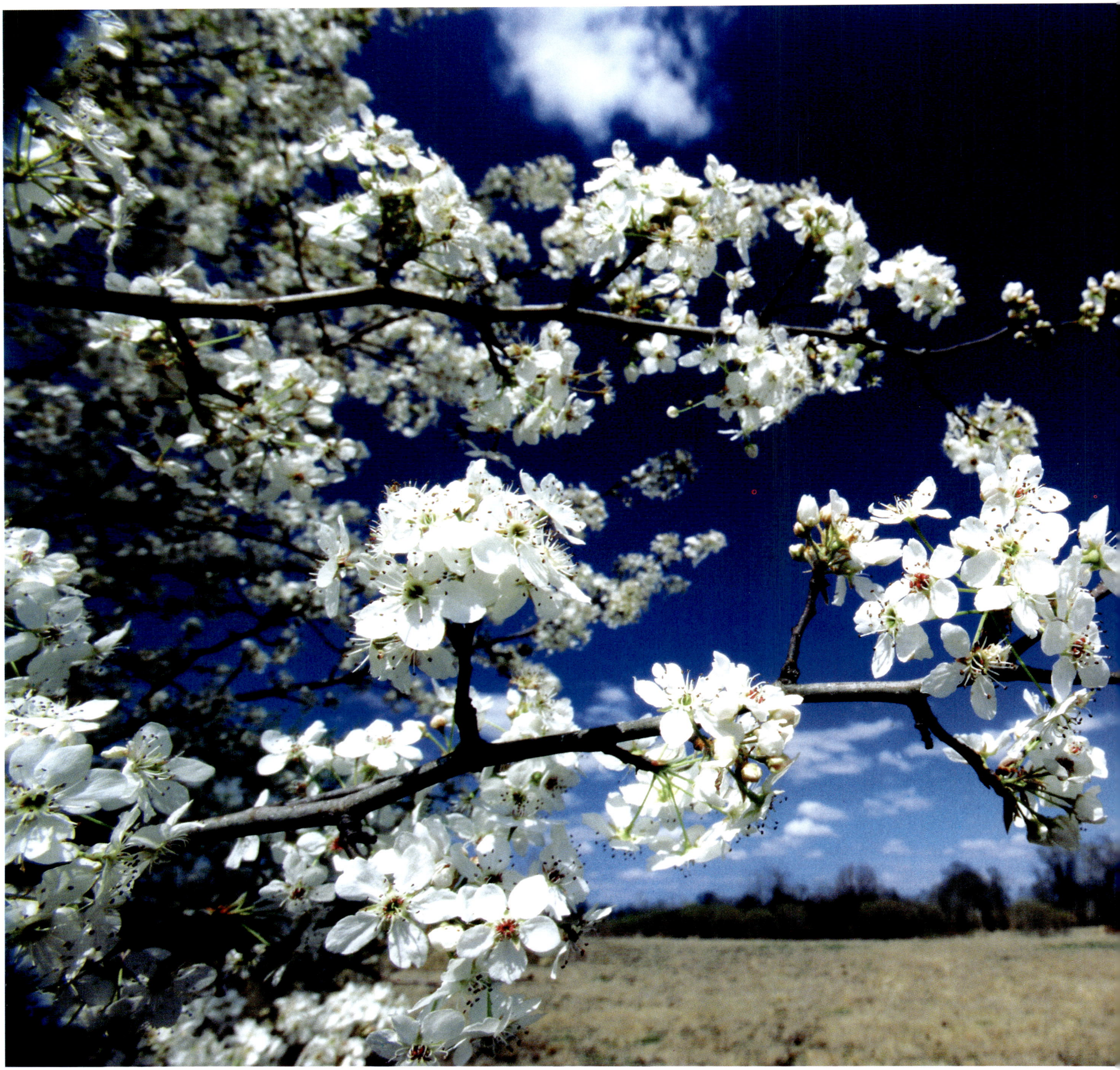

**OAKEN MOON**
June 2004
*500mm, f4@1/15*
The full moon rises behind water oak leaves.

**PROMISE OF SPRING**
March 2006
*17-35mm, f11@1/60*
The white flowers of the Chickasaw plum signal spring's arrival.

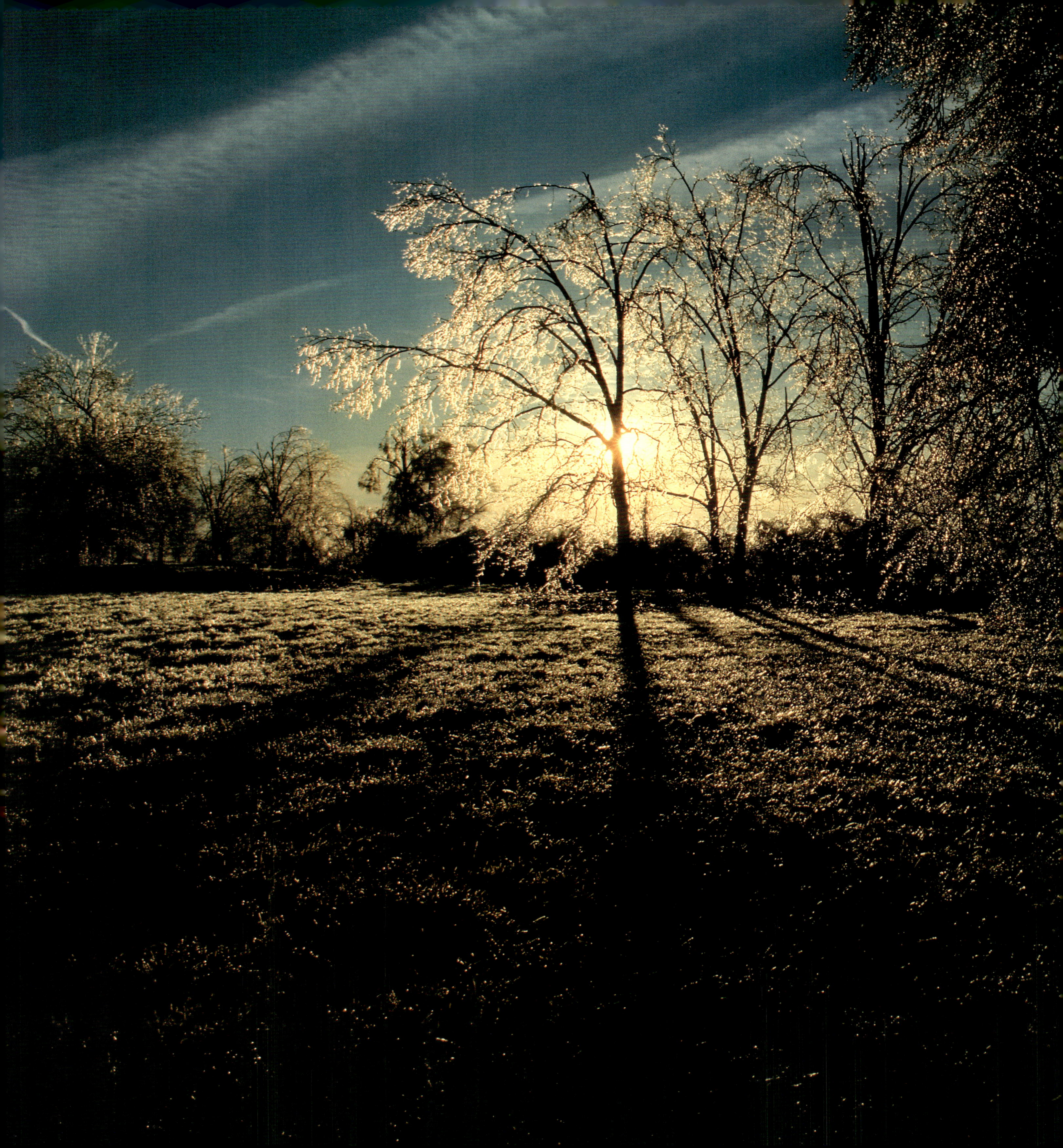

**AFTER THE STORM**
February 1988
*50mm, f11@1/125*

Ice-wrapped branches sparkle
in the sunrise.

**RESTING RAINBOW**
October 1983
*300mm, f4.5@1/250*

*A wood duck preens among the lotus plants.*

**RESERVOIR ROOST**
March 1991
*400mm, f3.5@1/125*

*Dead trees far from shore form a perfect roost for gregarious cormorants.*

**GREEN AROUND THE GILLS**
July 2004
*17-35mm f16@2 sec.*

*Mushroom gills are visible only from a bug's eye view.*

**LIFELINES**
July 2005
*60mm, f11@1/30*

*Late afternoon light illuminates the leaf of a palmetto and a tree frog at rest.*

**PHLOX PHLOOR**
April 2005
*17-35mm w/4x diopter, f16@2 sec.*

*Blue phlox carpets the forest floor.*

**DAWN'S DESIGN**
December 2005
*17-35mm w/split ND, f11@4 sec.*

*Morning light transforms a dead tree and small pond into a work of art.*

**BLUE SKY SPECIAL**
April 2006
*17-35mm, f22@1/30*

*Mustard greens served fresh, with a side order of puffy white clouds.*

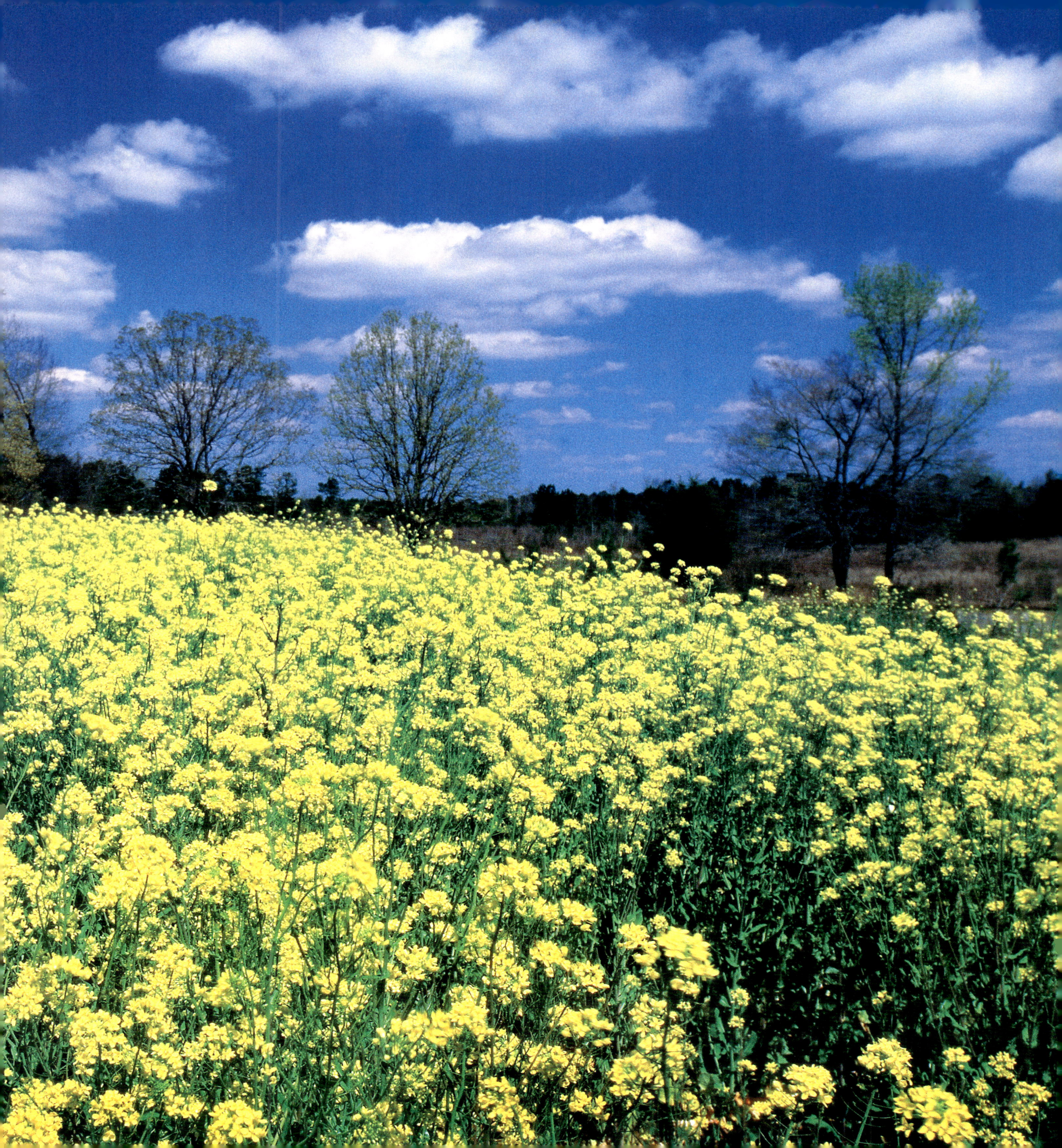

**CRESCENT PINE**
November 1993
*105mm, f2.8@1/30*

*The crescent moon rests in a pine tree near the Ross Barnett Reservoir.*

**MOVE ON**
May 2005
*500mm w/2x TC, f4@1/125*

*A great egret gets too close to a red-winged blackbird's nesting area.*

### WEB SITE LIGHT
June 2005
*17–35mm, f11@1/30*

*A dew-covered spider web glistens in the early morning light.*

**HAWKEYE**
December 1985
*400mm, f3.5@1/500*

*A northern harrier hovers over the marsh in search of prey.*

**STAR OF BETHLEHEM**
August 1990
*105mm, f11@1/8*

*The unassuming Star of Bethlehem rests on the forest floor.*

**DOGBANE AFTERNOON**
August 2004
*60mm, f11@1/8*

*Dogbane leaf beetles munch on milkweed leaves.*

**CATTAIL DAWN**
June 2005
*60mm, f8@1/30*

*A quiet pond forms the backdrop for a portrait of cattails.*

**MERGANSER MIST**
December 2005
*500mm, f4@1/125*
*Hooded mergansers cruise through the mist.*

**SPRING REVIVAL**
April 2006
*17-35mm, f8@1/60*
*Dogwood and redbud trees reach for the heavens.*

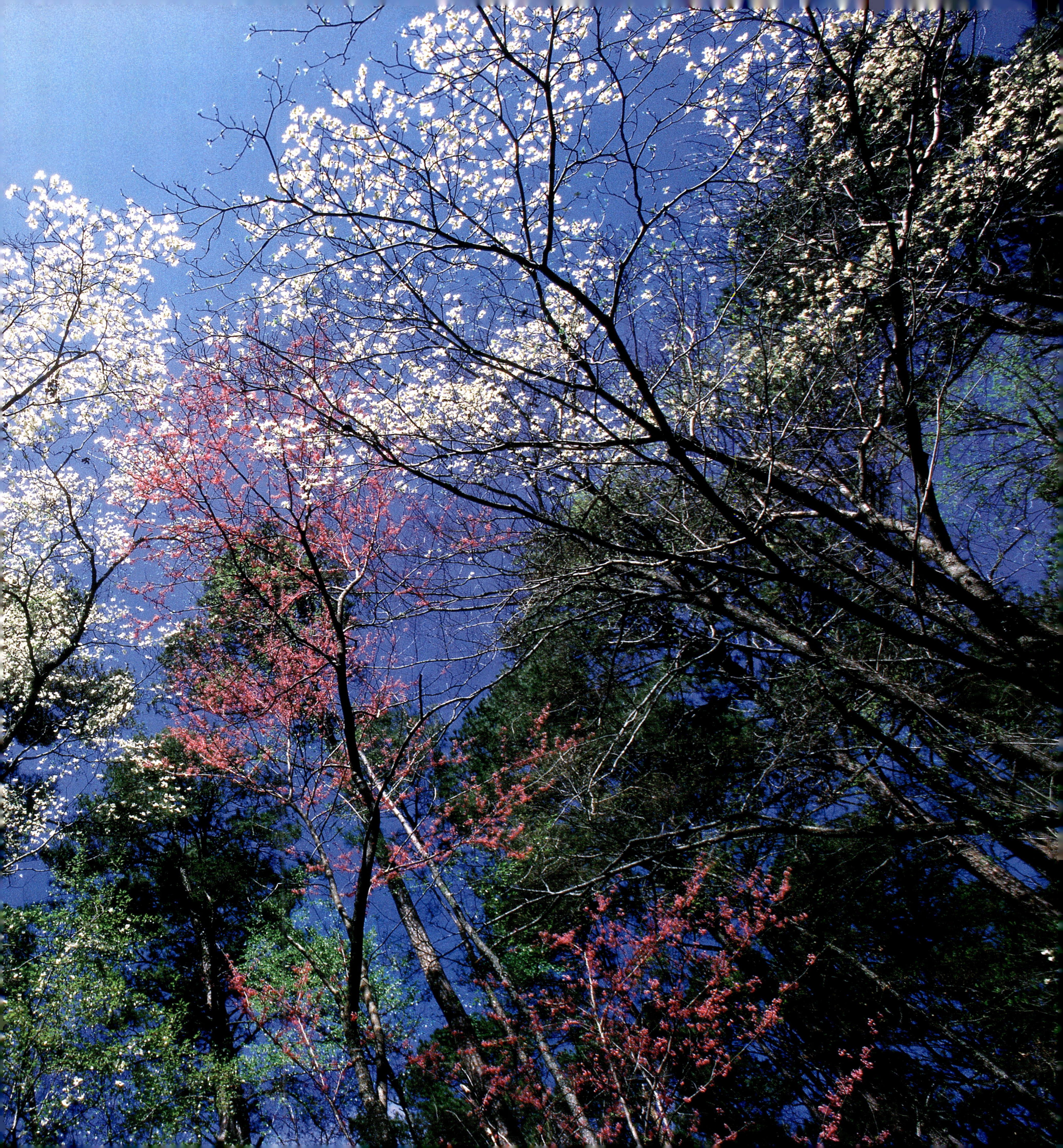

**UP AND AWAY**
April 2006
*500mm w/2xTC, f8@1/250*

*A bald eagle takes flight near Lake Caroline.*

### LOW PROFILE
June 1989
*400mm, f3.5@1/250*

*A family of Canada geese lies low,
hoping to avoid detection by predators.*

**WEB'S EYE**
September 2002
*105mm, f8@1/500*

*Sunrise burns the center of a dew-covered web.*

"MORE!"
May 2005
*60mm w/strobe, f22@1/125*

*Young Carolina wrens beg for food.*

**BURNING DAYLIGHT**
October 2005
*17-35mm w/split ND, f11@1/125*

*Sunrise melts the morning fog.*

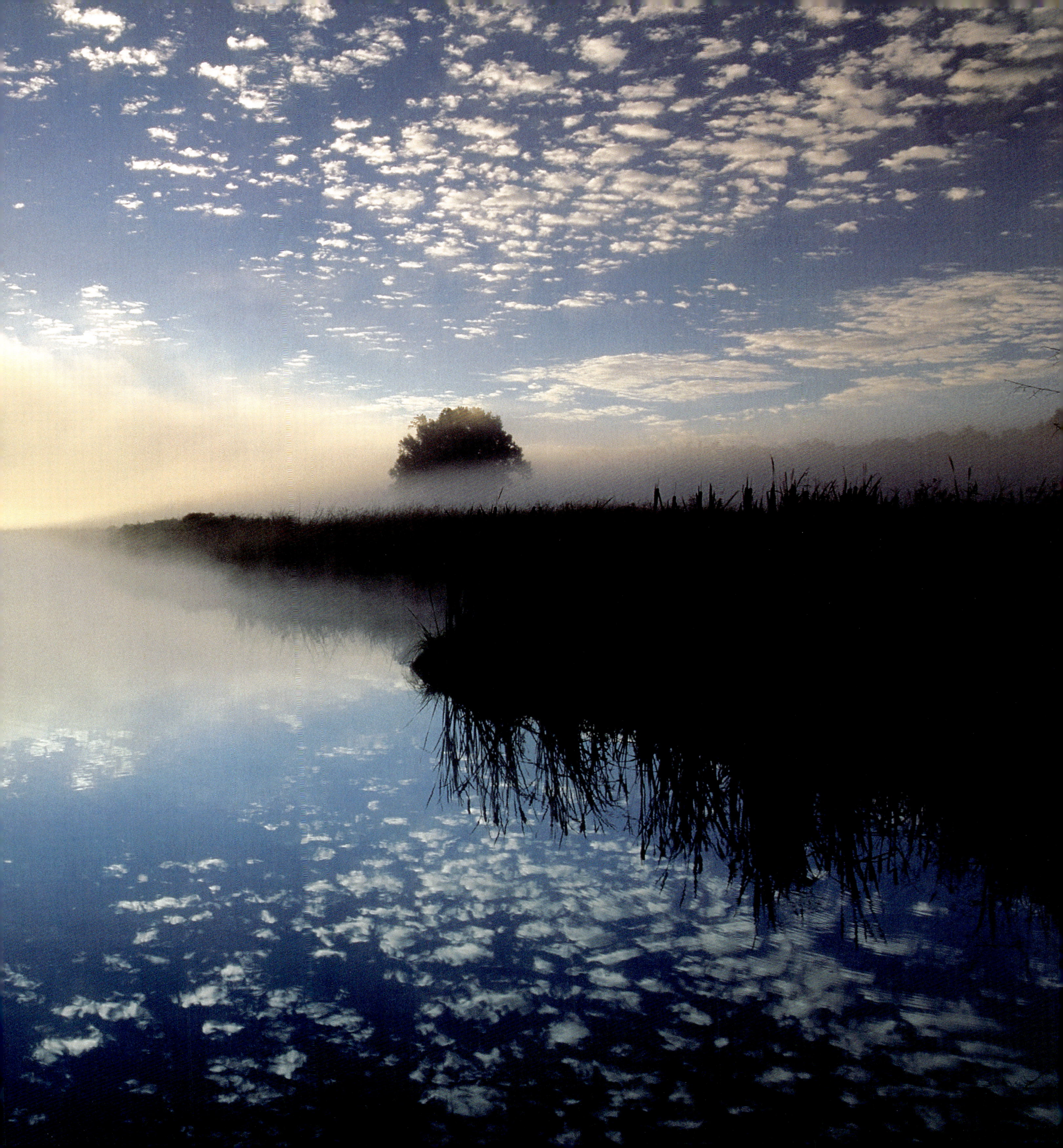

**PASSION MARKS**
February 1986
*70–210mm, f4@1/30*

*Airline contrails form a pattern that speaks of amazing grace.*

**LAST LIGHT**
December 1988
*400mm f3.5@1/30*

*A white-tailed deer follows a doe at the edge of a field at "dark-thirty."*

**SPRING SING**
April 2002
*500mm, f4@1/125*

*A common yellowthroat sings an invitation to females in his territory.*

**LOTUS**
June 1999
*400mm, f3.5@1/500*

*A creamy lotus bloom unfolds in the morning light.*

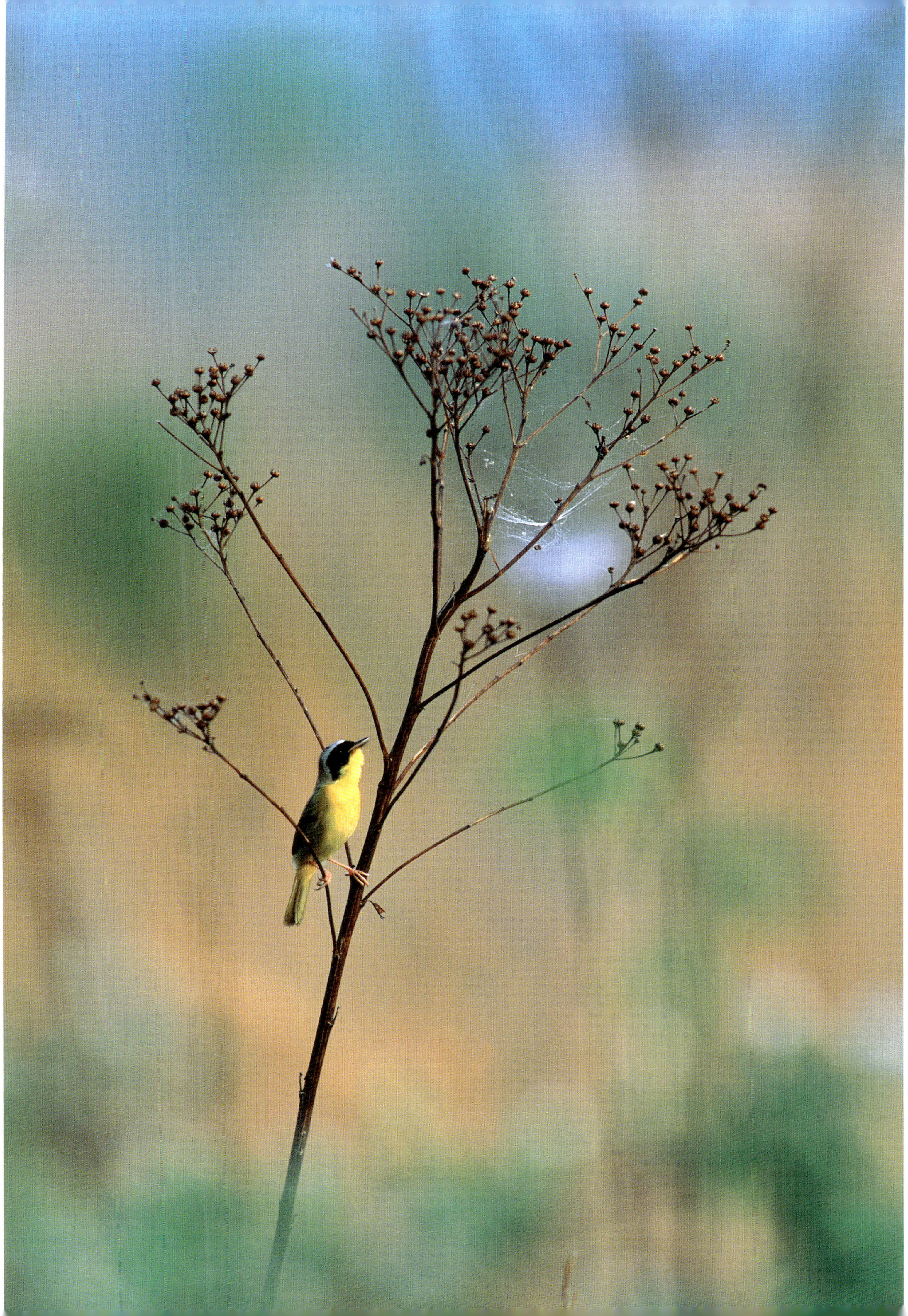

**MADISON COUNTY DAWN**
May 2005
*500mm w/2x TC, f8@1/60*

*The rising sun is a burning ball over the misty Pearl River swamp.*

**REDWING MORN**
May 2005
*500mm w/2x TC, f8@1/500*

*A red-winged blackbird calls
from the cattails.*

**SUBDEWED**
September 2003
*60mm, f11@1/4*

*A twelve-spotted skimmer frozen by the dew awaits the freeing rays of the sun.*

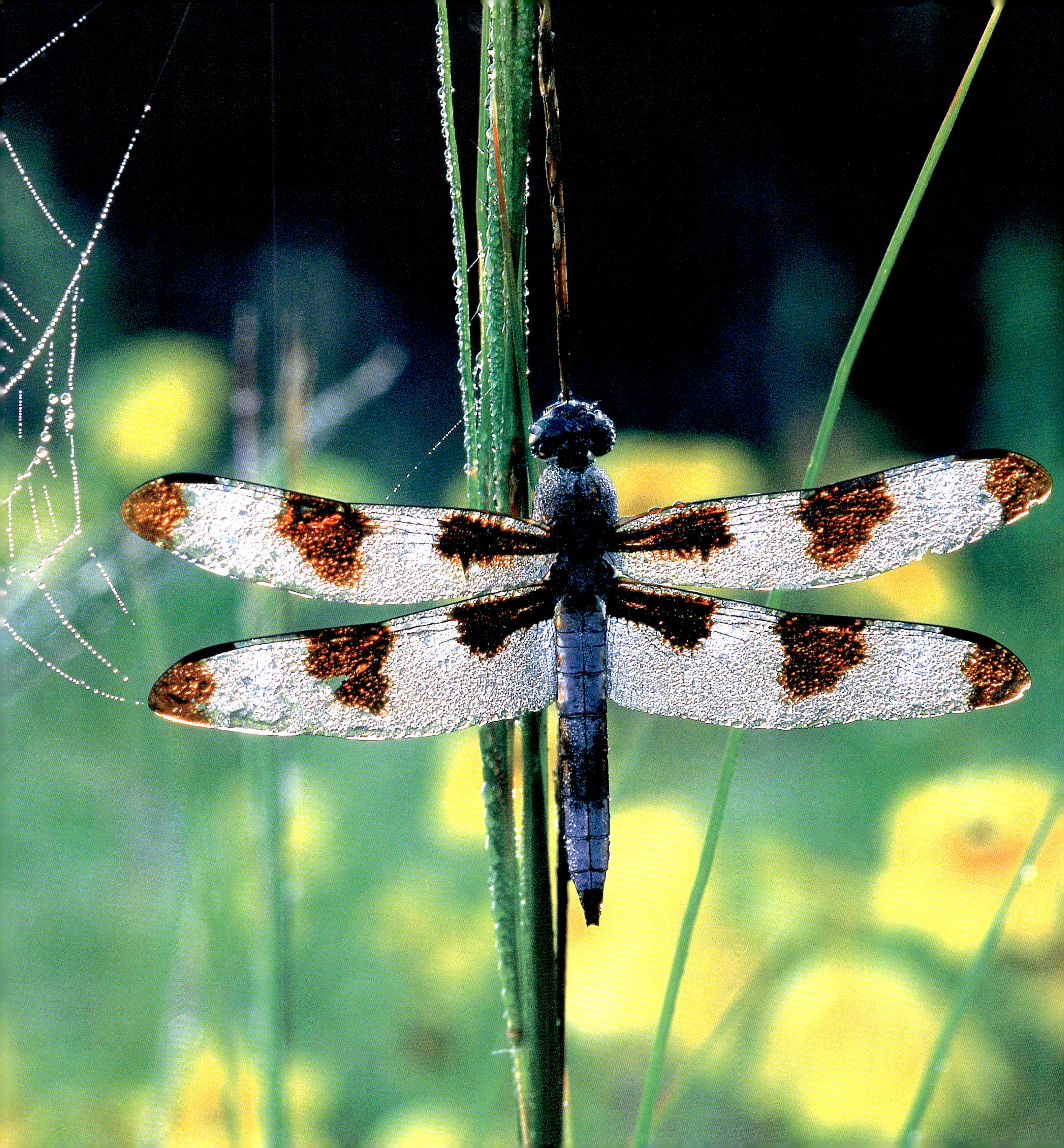

**MOURNING FLIGHT**
January 1999
*400mm, f3.5@1/250*

*Mourning doves head toward feeding grounds.*

**"WHOOO'S THERE?"**
April 2006
*500mm w/2x TC, f8@1/8*

*Still in the nest, a young great horned owl watches for activity at dusk.*

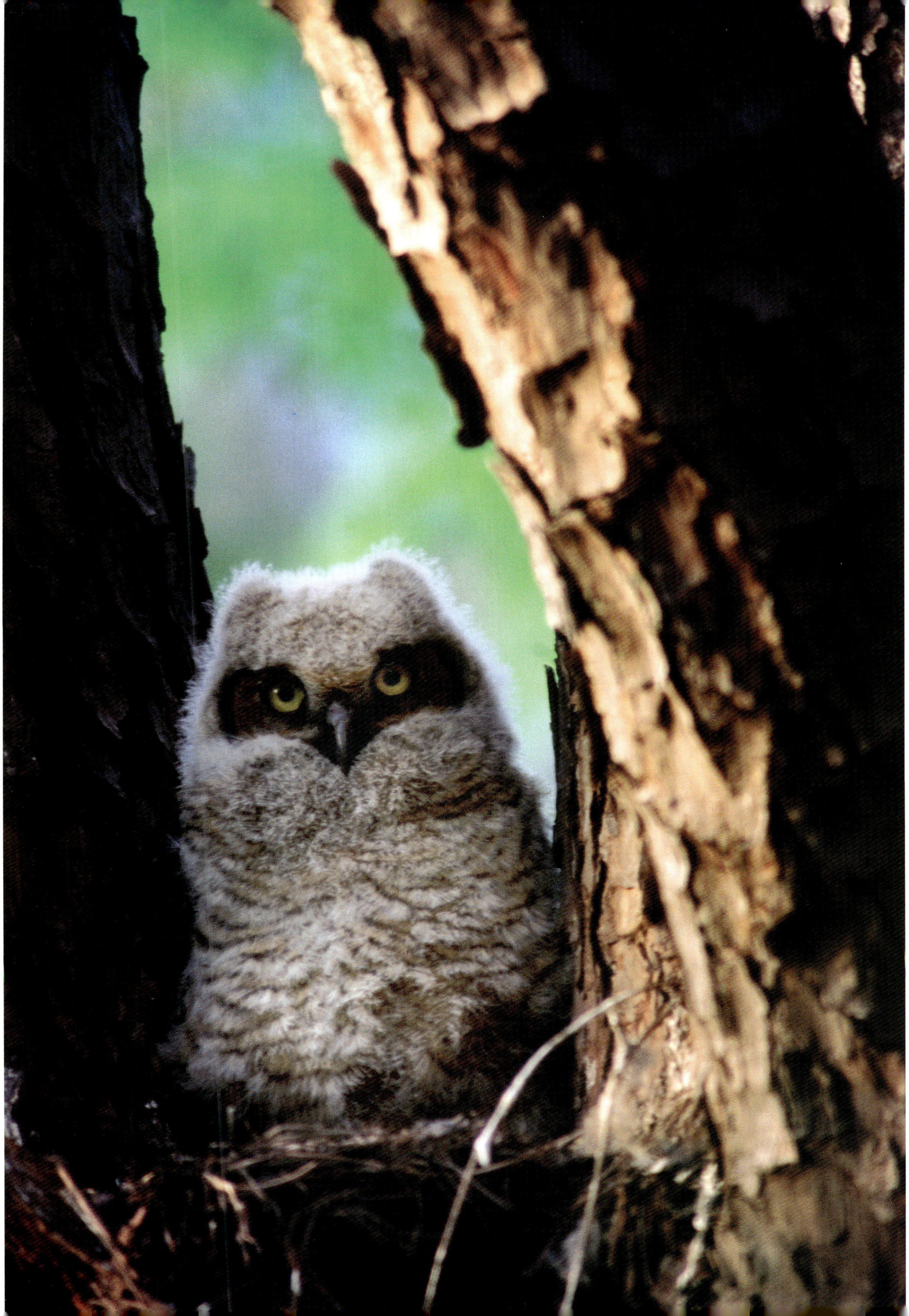

**LOST RABBIT SUNRISE**
June 2004

*17-35mm, f22@1/2*

*Cypress trees stand guard at the water's edge at the Lost Rabbit community.*

**TANGLE OF TEARS**
August 2003
*60mm, f16@1/8*

*A dew-covered web drapes vervain, forming a string of jewels in the early morning light.*

**COYOTE UGLY**
November 2005
*500mm, f4@1/60*

*A coyote holds the remains of "something" in its jaws.*

**SCAVENGER HUNT**
September 1992
*400mm, f3.5 @1000*

*Black vultures silhouetted at sunset.*

**CHEROKEE ROSE**
April 2005
*60mm, f5.6@1/15*

*The papery white texture of the Cherokee rose is heightened as it blooms.*

**IN SEASON**
June 2003
*105mm, f16@1/4*

*Blackberries bloom in prickly surroundings.*

**BLACK DUSK**
November 2005
*17-35mm, f11@1/30*

*A stormy sunset colors a cypress swamp near the Big Black River.*

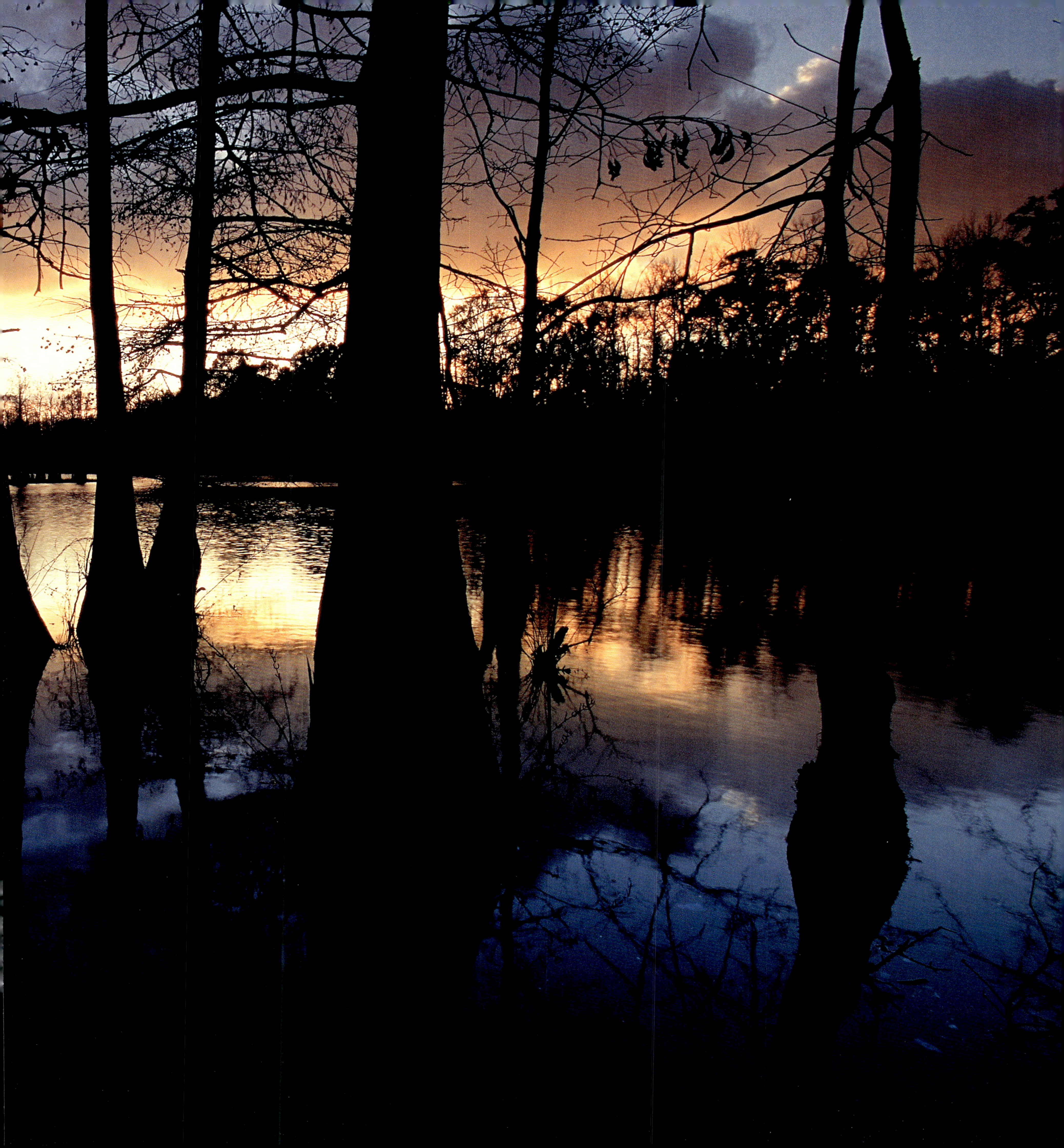

**BUCKEYE BOUQUET**
September 1984
*105mm, f11@1/60*

*A buckeye butterfly dines on sunflowers.*

**ABOVE THE SUN**
May 2005
*500mm, f4@1/250*

*An anhinga leaves its resting place at sunrise.*

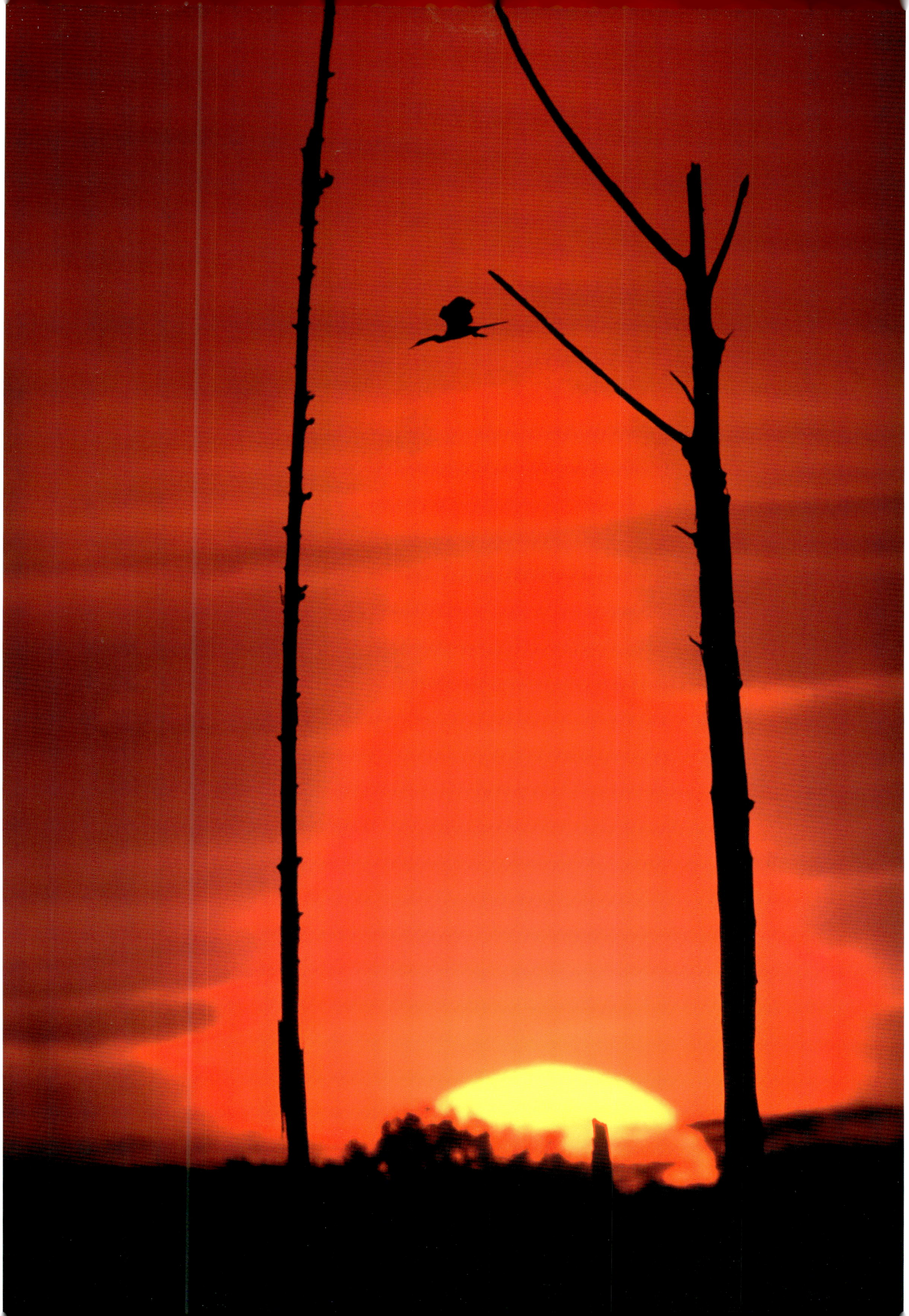

**SILVER SEEDS**
March 2006
*60mm, f8@1/30*

*Silver maple seedlings glisten after a spring rain.*

**SHEDDING THE PAST**
July 2001
*60mm, f8@1/4*

*A grass spider sheds its skin in early morning dew.*

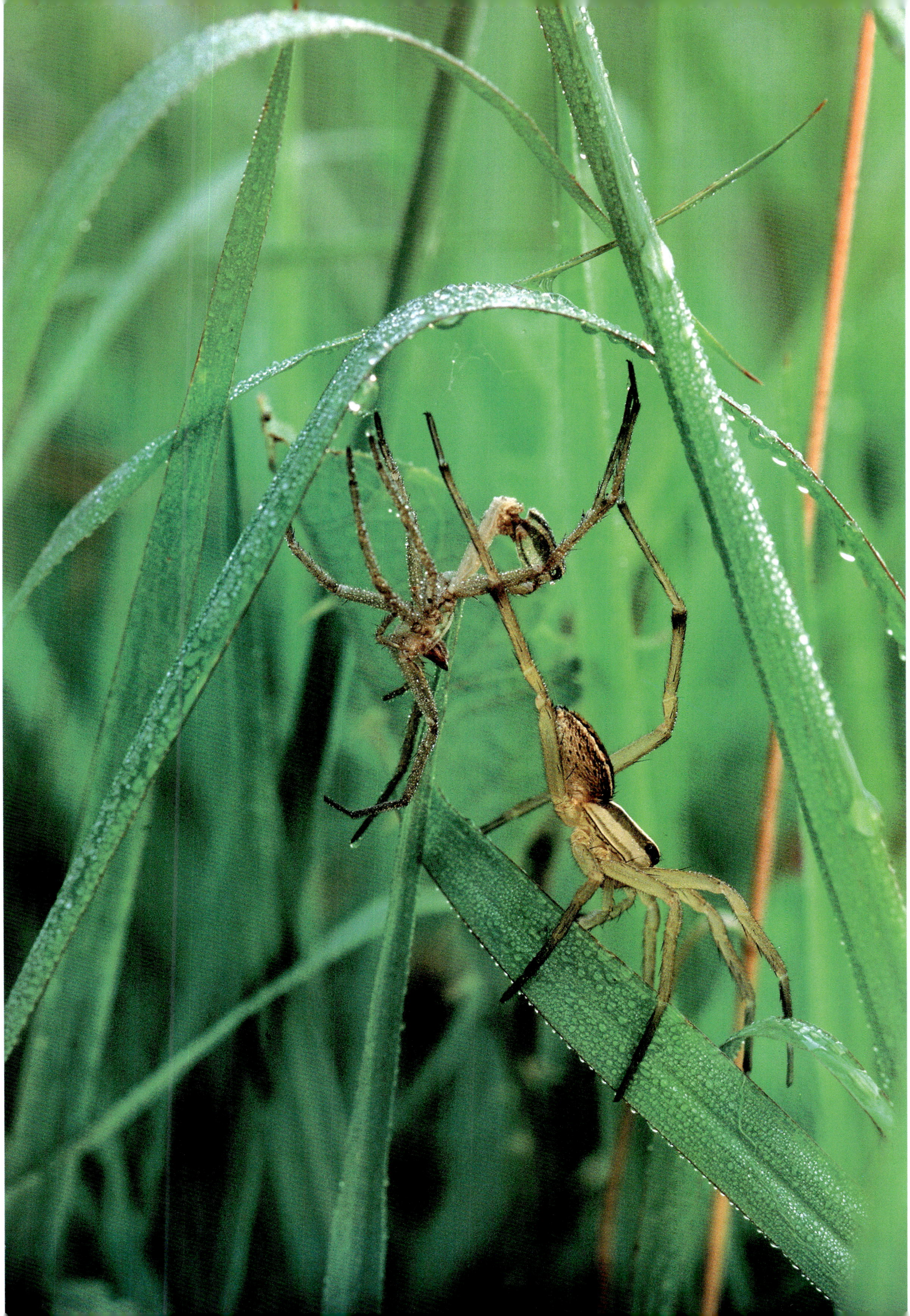

**CYPRESS SWAMP IMPRESSIONS**
August 2004
*17-35mm, f8@1/30*

*A cypress swamp filled with duckweed provides the perfect canvas for reflections.*

**LOTUS LEAF LIGHT**
June 2004
*17–35mm, f4@1/30*

*Sunrise reflected in a pool
of water cradled by a lotus leaf.*

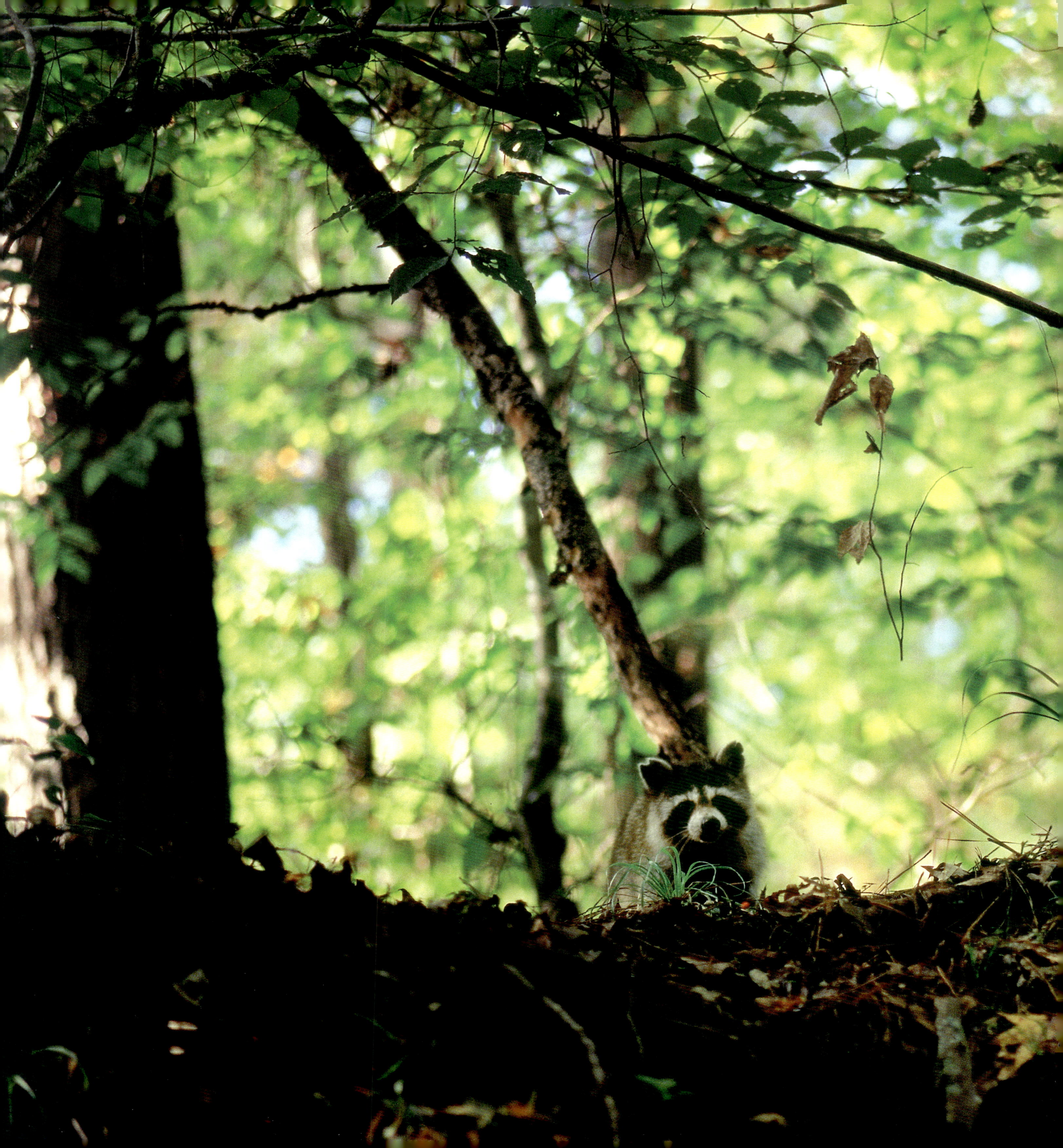

**"CREEK-A-BOO, I SEE YOU!"**
December 1994
*24mm, f4@1/60*

*An inquisitive raccoon peers over the edge of Bear Creek.*

**UPWARD**
November 1986
*400mm, f3.5@1/500*

*A gadwall makes a hurried departure from a flooded swamp.*

**'GATOR GROWL**
June 2004
*500mm, f4@1/125*

*An alligator claims a log as his own.*

**BACKDROP**
June 2005
*17–35mm w/split ND, f4@1/4*

*A small lake reflects nature's infinite glory.*

**HANGING BY A THREAD**
June 2005
*60mm, f4@1/60*

*A damselfly is suspended from
the remnants of a spider web.*

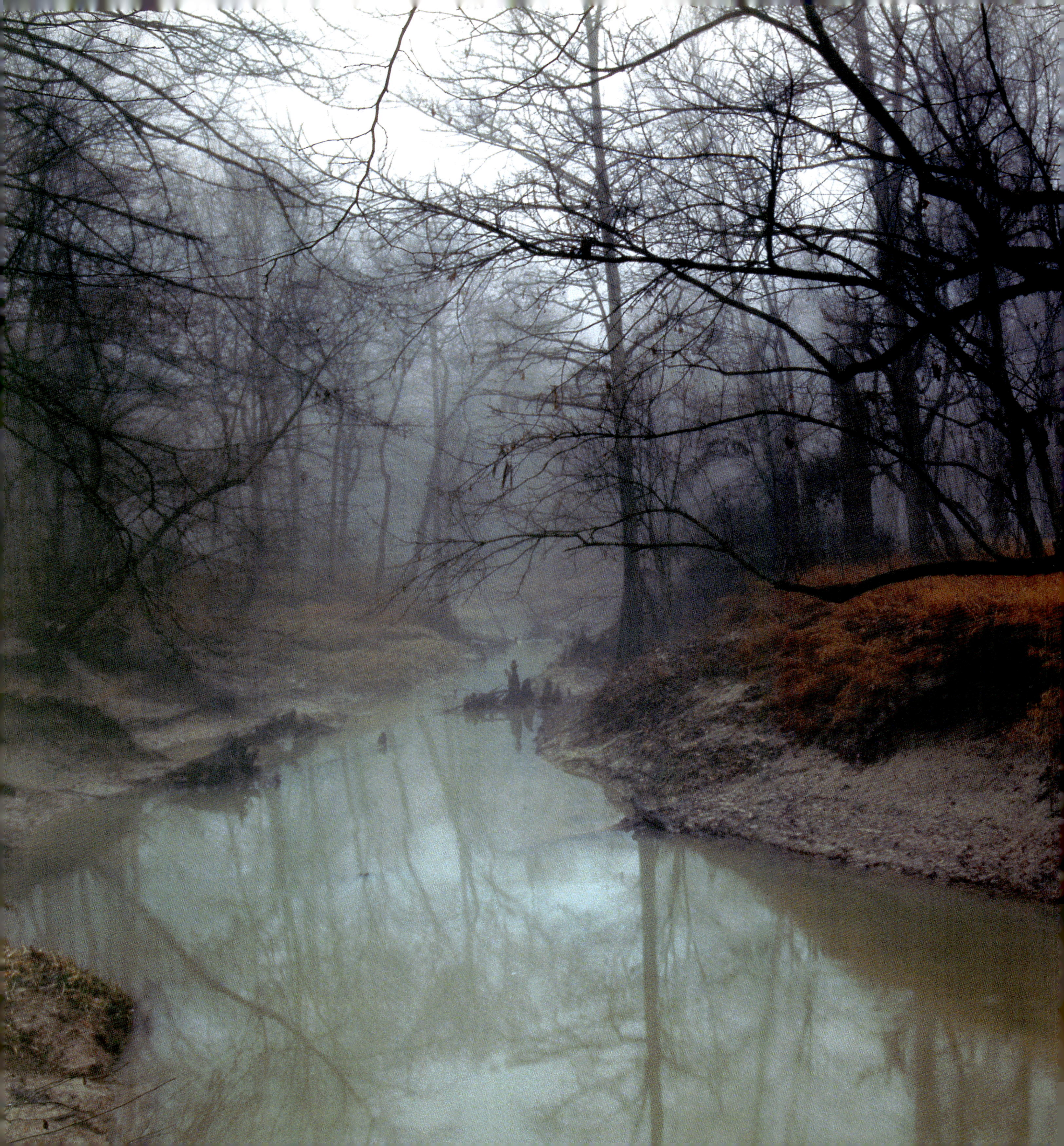

**BOGUE CHITTO MIST**
January 2006
*17-35mm w/split ND, f22@4sec.*

*Morning mist shrouds
Bogue Chitto Creek.*

**STOPLIGHT**
May 2003
*500mm, f4@1/250*

*A gray rat snake warns of a pending strike.*

**HUNG OUT TO DRY**
September 2003
*60mm, f16@1/15*

*Gulf fritillaries dry in the early morning sun.*

**SPANISH SNOW**
December 1996
*180mm, f5.6@1/60*

*A rare snowfall covers Spanish moss.*

**CYPRESS LIGHT**
January 2005
*180mm, f11@1/15*

*Cypress knees glow in the
late evening light.*

**WINGED WELCOME**
November 2004
*17–35mm w/split ND, f2.8@1/30*

*Red-winged blackbirds
take flight at sunrise.*

**NATURAL LINES**
October 1991
*180mm, f11@1/60*

*The reflections of grasses and
snags form patterns in still water.*

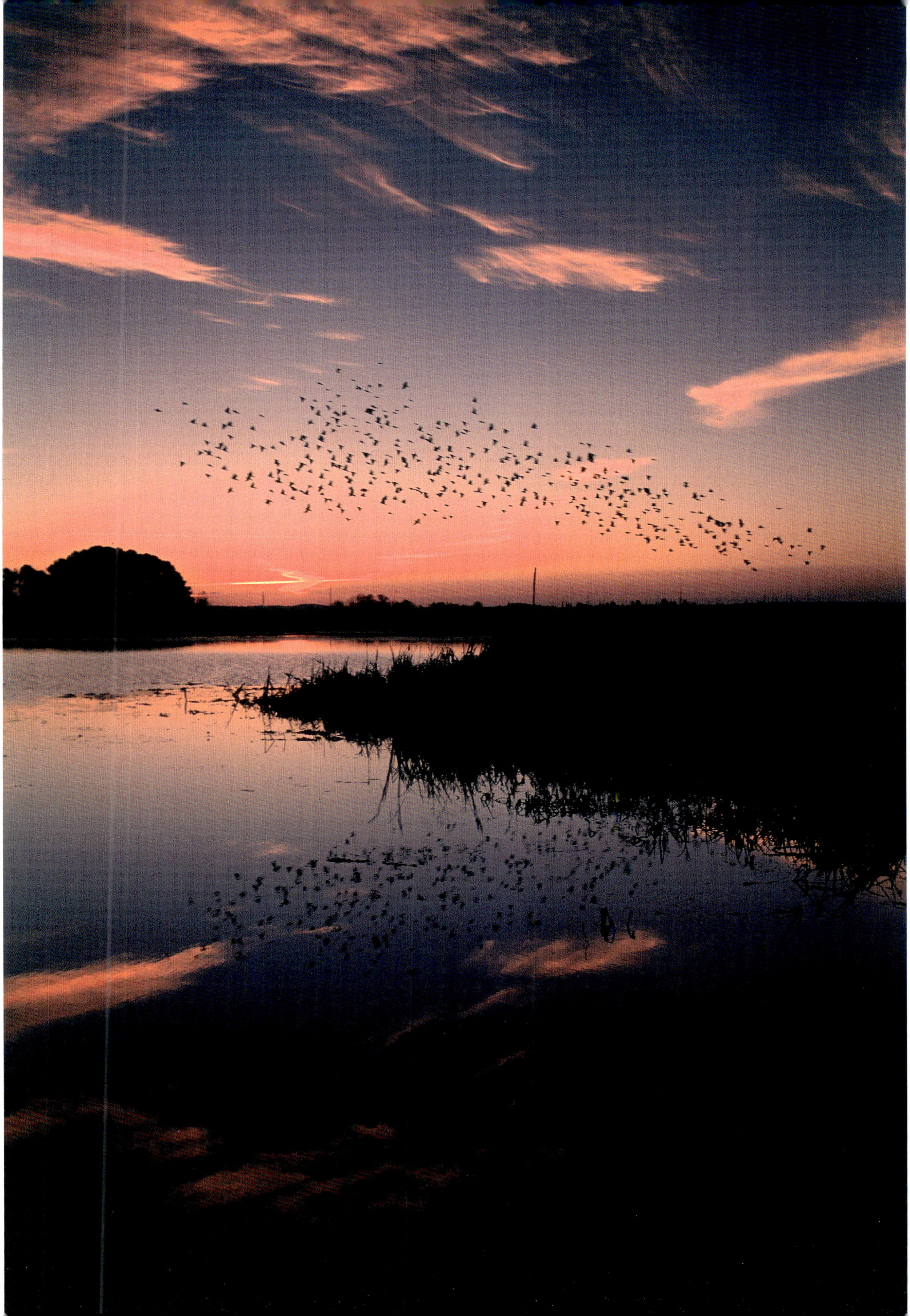

# IN OUR OWN BACKYARD

Every day has a sunrise, but no two are the same.

It's not so different with a familiar place. Just when we become comfortable in its rhythms and confident we know what to expect, we find it still has the ability to surprise.

A backyard can sometimes feel too small, too ordinary, but if we stop to look around, to truly see the majesty and beauty around us, we realize that we don't need to look any further to catch a glimpse of something bigger, something extraordinary.

Even here in Madison County, Mississippi, a locale so familiar and comfortable, a place so near and dear, there will always be cause for wonder.

**SKY'S THE LIMIT**
January 1988
*50mm, f8@1/125*

*Sunset over the Ross Barnett Reservoir forms the multi-colored backdrop for a great egret headed to roost.*

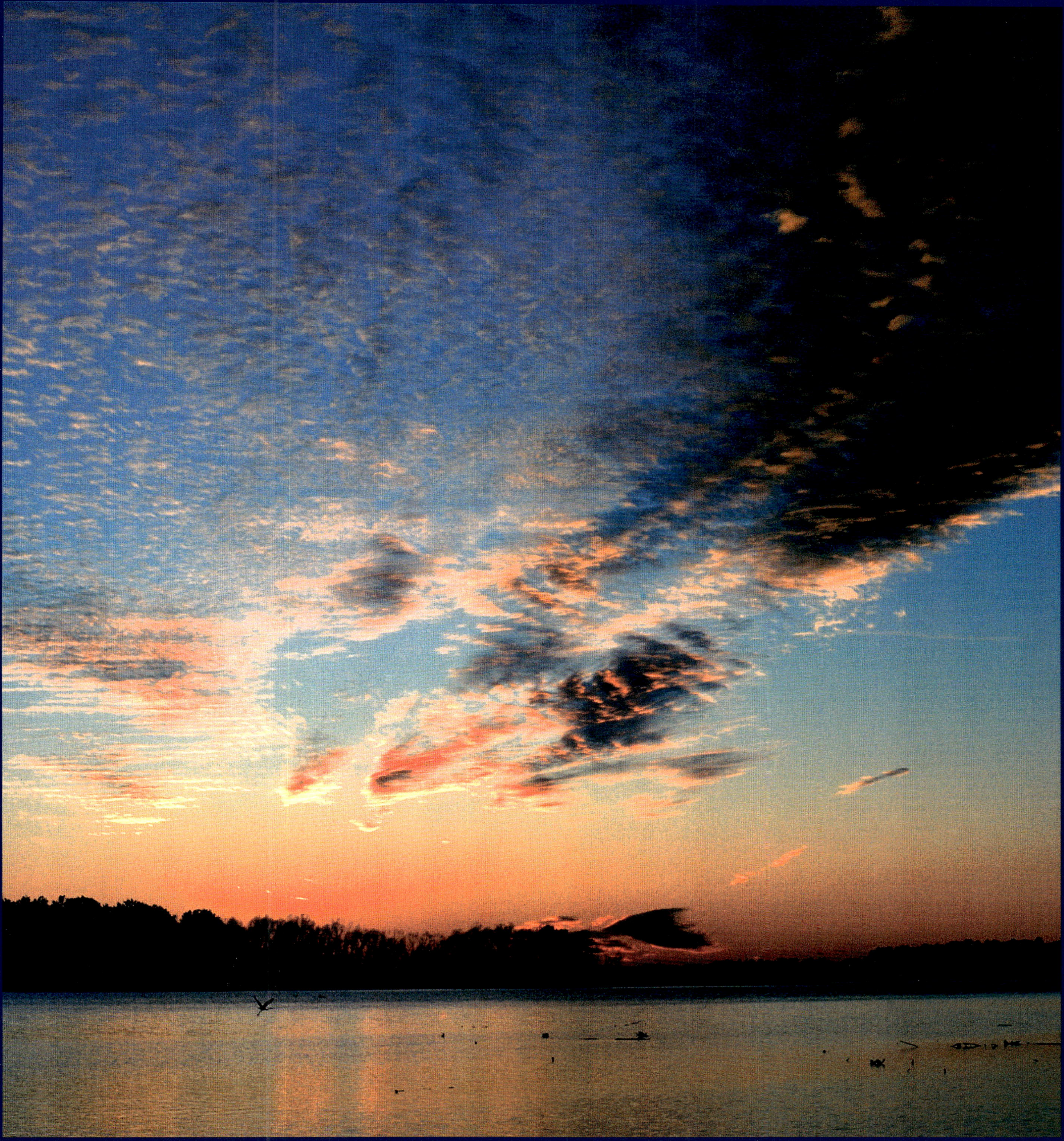

# MOMENTS IN MADISON COUNTY

People often ask me if I set out in search of a particular shot or if I just step into the wilderness and see what I can find. While I usually have an idea in mind before I go, I am all too familiar with the unpredictability of nature. If an unexpected shot presents itself, whatever I had originally planned is usually forgotten.

Working in Madison County has taught me that even the most familiar place has the ability to surprise. The images on these pages illustrate not only the diversity of flora and fauna in Madison County, but also the photography techniques used to capture them. Some I set out to shoot, some were fortunate accidents, but each one represents a magical moment in Madison County.

---

**MORNING COMMUTE** *(Pages 10-11)*
September 2002
*500mm, f4@1/1000*

*The Canada geese on a lake near our house departed every morning at 6:45 on the dot. Getting into position and ready to shoot was an easy assignment. A beautiful sunrise, on the other hand, was anything but predictable. I watched their morning commute for weeks, until finally, the perfect pass in the perfect light. If only the commute from Madison County down I-55 were this inspiring.*

---

**WALNUT REFLECTIONS** *(Page 15)*
March 1998
*24mm, f22@1/8*

*This shot of quiet Walnut Creek was the only image I captured in Madison County in all of 1998. That year took me to California, Peru, Canada, Florida, Alaska, New Hampshire, Vermont, back to Peru, and finally to Belize. In the midst of that busy schedule, my wife, Marlo, and I were married in Machu Picchu, Peru, that spring. It's probably no coincidence that my sole photo taken at home captured a moment of quiet reflection.*

**WEB OF PEARLS**  *(Page 27)*
October 2004
*60mm, f8@1/4*

*I wanted to shoot the Pearl River on a foggy morning but couldn't find a good vantage point. As I searched for just the right place, I spotted this spider web covered with dew, and abandoned my river shot to explore the possibilities. I changed lenses, set up this shot, looked through the viewfinder, and saw another example of serendipity at work.*

**MISTY MOONSET**  *(Page 28)*
October 2004
*180mm, f4@1/60*

*Dawn was approaching, a mist was forming, the full moon was setting over a quiet field, and a wonderful chill was in the air. My goal was to capture the whole scene—the whole feeling—on film. I had only to wait until the light values were right to keep the moon from burning out. That moment soon arrived. You will just have to imagine the chill.*

**LUNCH BREAK**  *(Page 35)*
June 2004
*500mm, f4@1/30*

*I was shooting a brochure for Lost Rabbit, a residential development on the Ross Barnett Reservoir. I only had a few days to capture the essence of the over 200-acre site. One of the thoughts I was asked to communicate was "family friendly community." I happened upon an indigo bunting nest, set up my blind, and left it for the birds to grow accustomed to. I came back the following day and waited until the mother arrived with a fat katydid for her hungry babies. The shot didn't make the brochure, but seemed a natural for a book on family-friendly Madison County.*

**RESTING RAINBOW**  *(Page 52)*
October 1983
*300mm, f4.5@1/250*

*I was in my "frog's eye view" mode of pursuit, neck deep in a swamp and forcing my way through thick lotus plants, when I heard a splashing. I stopped and listened closely, then recognized the broken rhythm of a bird preening and bathing in the water. I made my way slowly, slowly to a spot where I could see. Much to my delight, it was a beautiful male wood duck surrounded by a vivid palette of dying lotus plants. This was one of my earliest shots taken at frog's eye view; I was thrilled to see the technique actually getting results.*

**LIFELINES**  (Page 55)
July 2005
*60mm, f11@1/30*

*Finding this image was easy. I looked out the window of my home office and there it was. The late afternoon light was shinning directly through a palmetto into my line of sight. I noticed a dark spot on the leaf and closer inspection revealed a green tree frog resting there. I grabbed my camera, stepped out the front door, and had the shot I wanted.*

---

**MOVE ON**  (Page 61)
May 2005
*500mm w/2x TC, f4@1/125*

*I was spectator to a feeding frenzy at a small, swampy body of water that was slowly drying up. Herons and egrets were coming and going at a record pace. As they sailed in, red-winged blackbirds nesting nearby came out to harass those who ventured too close. I captured one shot in the golden light of a balmy, misty morning.*

---

**SPRING REVIVAL**  (Pages 68-69)
April 2006
*17-35mm, f8@1/60*

*I was driving along the Natchez Trace Parkway on a spring day bursting with life. The fresh green leaves and colorful flowers seemed to grow and deepen in intensity before my eyes. I stopped the car when I spotted two large dogwoods in full bloom, their white flowers and delicate branches encircling a redbud tree. Stepping beneath those glorious trees felt like stepping into a church. The trees stretched toward the heavens as I composed a pictorial hymn.*

---

**BURNING DAYLIGHT**  (Pages 74-75)
October 2005
*17-35mm w/split ND, f11@1/125*

*The morning was cold, clear, and perfectly still. The low-lying morning fog was dissipating as I walked to the water's edge. As the sun rose, the mood changed. The dramatic effect of water, clouds, and light came together to create an image of power and peace.*

**MADISON COUNTY DAWN**  *(Page 80)*
May 2005
*500mm w/2x TC, f8@1/60*

*The day before I had spotted this tree and staked out where the sun would rise. I returned in the dark before dawn to capture what I hoped would be a striking shot. The sun appeared to blossom as it emerged through the softening mist. The resulting red ball was even more dramatic than I'd hoped—one of the rare moments when nature actually cooperated with my plans.*

**SUBDEWED**  *(Pages 82-83)*
September 2003
*60mm, f11@1/4*

*Roaming dew-covered fields in the early morning before sunrise is a favorite activity, especially when I stumble upon little jewels of nature like this one. Finding this twelve-spotted skimmer and spider web covered in dew next to one another was a small miracle. The light of dawn was behind my subject and the yellow flowers added "pop" to the composition. I paid careful attention to the surrounding vegetation—one careless move and the whole thing would come tumbling down.*

**"CREEK-A-BOO, I SEE YOU!"**  *(Pages 100-101)*
December 1994
*24mm, f4@1/60*

*I was standing in the shallow waters of Bear Creek when I heard a rustling above. I looked up and saw a raccoon peering down at me. I pulled the camera off of the tripod and captured one shot before the curious coon disappeared. There was no time to change lenses from my wide-angle to a close-up, but when I saw the resulting image, I realized a better creative decision had been made for me.*

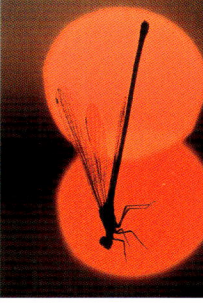

**BACKDROP**  *(Page 104)*          **HANGING BY A THREAD**  *(Page 105)*
June 2005                            June 2005
*17-35mm w/split ND filter, f4@1/4*   *60mm, f4@1/60*

*Taken only moments apart, these two shots are the perfect example of how the best plans can be overruled by serendipity. I composed the landscape shot over and over, moving and shooting again and again. As the sun peeked over the trees, I decided it was not going to be one of those "special" sunrises. I was disappointed until I looked right in front of me and saw a tiny damselfly, seemingly levitating in midair. Looking closer, I saw that an old, deteriorating spider web with just a few strands still intact was holding the tiny insect aloft. I switched to a macro lens and focused within inches of the web. The damselfly's positioning was perfect in front of the rising sun. I hand held the camera and shot as the sun's reflection gave me two glowing balls. It was a special sunrise after all.*

**GOLDEN GLIDE**
August 1997
*400mm, f3.5@1/125*

*White ibis glide over the
Pearl River swamp at dawn.*